BinaryCoder X

Programming Softwares

Dedication:

To the dreamers who weave visions in algorithms, the architects of the digital future, and the tireless explorers of the code-sculpted landscapes. This book is dedicated to the relentless spirits that breathe life into the binary, the ones who dare to imagine and shape the realms of possibility. May your keystrokes echo through the corridors of innovation, and may your code be a testament to the boundless potential within each line.

"Within the lines of code, a universe unfolds. 'Programming Softwares And How To Use Them' is your compass through the digital cosmos, where the language of creation echoes in every keystroke. Join me on this journey of discovery, where the art of programming becomes a doorway to boundless innovation." - BinaryCoder X

BinaryCoder X

Contents

1.

2.

3.

4.

5.

6.

7.

8.

9.

10.

11.

12.

13.

14.

15.

16.

17.

18.

19.

20.

21.

22.

Foreword

Foreword

In the labyrinth of zeros and ones, where imagination converges with logic, programming emerges as the alchemy that transforms ideas into digital reality. "Programming Softwares And How To Use Them" by BinaryCoder X is more than a guide; it is an invitation to traverse the landscape of programming tools and discover the symphony of creation that echoes through lines of code.

As we stand on the precipice of technological innovation, BinaryCoder X takes the helm, guiding us through a comprehensive exploration of the software ecosystem that fuels our digital ambitions. This book is a testament to the boundless potential of human ingenuity, encapsulating the essence of programming languages and the tools that breathe life into our collective imagination.

The digital realm is expansive, and within its vastness lies a multitude of programming languages and software tailored for diverse tasks. BinaryCoder X, a seasoned navigator through this realm, embarks on a compelling journey, unraveling the enigma of each programming software with clarity and purpose. From the foundations of IDEs to the intricacies of graphic design and the realm of databases, this book unfurls the sails of understanding, propelling us into the uncharted territories of coding mastery.

What makes this journey truly captivating is BinaryCoder X's unique ability to bridge the gap between the novice and the adept, between those who dream and those who craft. Whether you are a budding coder, a seasoned developer, or someone intrigued by the magic behind the screen, this book is an invaluable companion on your quest for programming enlightenment.

Through the pages of "Programming Softwares And How To Use Them," BinaryCoder X inspires us to transcend the ordinary, to embrace the challenge of programming, and to wield the tools of creation with finesse. The foreword is not merely an introduction; it is a call to adventure, an invocation to explore the realms of programming and harness the power of software to sculpt the digital future.

May this journey be as enlightening and exhilarating for you as it has been for BinaryCoder X. Welcome to a world where each line of code is a brushstroke on the canvas of innovation, and every software is a portal to endless possibilities.

BinaryCoder X

Preface

Preface

In the ever-evolving landscape of technology, where the lines between reality and the digital realm continue to blur, the art of programming stands as the bedrock of innovation. In this dynamic world, where ideas are transformed into lines of code and where every keystroke holds the potential to shape the future, understanding the myriad programming software available is nothing short of essential.

Welcome to "Programming Softwares And How To Use Them" by BinaryCoder X. This book is not just a guide; it's an odyssey into the heart of the digital universe, where programming languages are the dialects spoken by creators, engineers, and visionaries. BinaryCoder X takes you on a journey through the expansive realm of programming tools, unraveling the mysteries behind each software's interface, commands, and functionalities.

As we delve into the intricacies of programming, BinaryCoder X demystifies the complexities of a diverse array of software, from the stalwarts like Visual Studio Code and Python IDEs to the specialized tools such as AutoCAD and Adobe Creative Suite. Whether you're a seasoned developer seeking to master a new language or an aspiring coder taking the first steps into this mesmerizing realm, this book is your compass through the vast landscapes of programming.

Through meticulous exploration and clear instructions, BinaryCoder X offers insights into the practical use of programming software. Each chapter unfolds the capabilities of a specific tool, guiding you through its features, functionalities, and the artistry of crafting code within its domain. From the precision of database management to the visual symphony of graphic design, this book embarks on an expedition that celebrates the diversity of programming applications.

So, fasten your seatbelts as we embark on this expedition into the heart of programming software. Whether you're a curious novice or a seasoned coder, "Programming Softwares And How To Use Them" is your passport to the vibrant and ever-evolving world of programming. Let the journey begin, and may your code compile seamlessly and your creativity flow endlessly.

BinaryCoder   X

Acknowledgement

Acknowledgments

As I stand at the crossroads of code and creativity, penning the final lines of "Programming Softwares And How To Use Them," I am overwhelmed with gratitude for the countless hands that have shaped this endeavor into reality. This journey has been nothing short of an odyssey, and its completion is a testament to the collaborative spirit that defines the world of programming.

First and foremost, my deepest appreciation goes to the coding community — an extraordinary collective of minds that breathe life into the digital realm. Your passion, commitment, and willingness to share knowledge have been the guiding stars that lit the path through the complexities of programming languages and software intricacies.

To the mentors and trailblazers who have illuminated my understanding, your wisdom has been the compass that steered this book's course. Your generosity in sharing insights and experiences has enriched these pages and, in turn, the journeys of those who seek to unravel the mysteries of programming.

A heartfelt thank you to the tireless developers, engineers, and designers who sculpted the programming tools explored in these chapters. Your dedication to crafting intuitive and powerful software has not only shaped industries but has also empowered countless individuals to bring their ideas to life.

I extend my gratitude to the readers — the adventurers poised to embark on the journey within these pages. Your curiosity fuels the engine of progress, and it is my hope that this book serves as a reliable guide on your expedition through the realms of programming.

To the editorial team and everyone behind the scenes, your meticulous work has transformed this manuscript into a polished narrative. Your commitment to excellence has elevated the content and ensured that it resonates with both the novice and the seasoned coder.

Lastly, to my family and friends, who have stood by me throughout this creative pilgrimage — your support, encouragement, and understanding have been the bedrock upon which this endeavor thrived. Your unwavering belief in the power of programming and the potential of every aspiring coder has fueled my determination to make this book a beacon of knowledge.

In conclusion, the completion of "Programming Softwares And How To Use Them" is a shared victory, a culmination of collective effort, and a celebration of the indomitable spirit of the programming community. May this book inspire, educate, and spark the flame of curiosity in every reader who ventures into its pages.

BinaryCoder   X

1

Operating System (e.g., Windows, macOS, Linux)

To program for an operating system (OS), you typically use development tools, libraries, and frameworks that are specific to the target OS. Here's a high-level overview for Windows, macOS, and Linux:

Windows:

1. **Development Environment:**
   - Use an integrated development environment (IDE) like Visual Studio for Windows development.

2. **Programming Languages:**
   - Choose a language compatible with Windows development, such as C++, C#, or .NET languages.

3. **APIs and Libraries:**

- Utilize Windows API (Application Programming Interface) for system-level interactions.

- Explore libraries like Win32 API for GUI applications.

4. **.NET Framework:**

- If using .NET languages, leverage the .NET framework for Windows application development.

macOS:

1. **Development Environment:**

- Xcode is the primary IDE for macOS development.

2. **Programming Languages:**

- Swift and Objective-C are the primary languages for macOS development.

3. **Cocoa Framework:**

- Use the Cocoa framework for creating macOS applications, including GUI elements.

4. **Interface Builder:**

- Interface Builder, integrated with Xcode, helps design user interfaces.

Linux:

1. **Development Environment:**
    - Linux development often occurs in various text editors (e.g., Vim, Emacs) or IDEs like VSCode.

2. **Programming Languages:**
    - Choose languages like C, C++, Python, or others based on your application needs.

3. **System Libraries:**
    - Interact with the Linux kernel and system libraries for low-level operations.

4. **Desktop Environment Integration:**
    - For desktop applications, consider toolkits like GTK or Qt for GUI development.

Cross-Platform Development:

1. **Cross-Platform Libraries:**
    - Use cross-platform libraries and frameworks like Qt, wxWidgets, or Electron for writing code that works on multiple OSes.

2. **Containerization:**

   - Utilize container technologies like Docker for creating portable applications.

3. **Virtualization:**

   - Employ virtual machines or emulators to test your code on different operating systems.

Remember, the specifics of your approach depend on your project's requirements and the type of application you are developing. Always refer to the documentation and guidelines provided by the respective OS or development tools.

2

Word Processing Software (e.g., Microsoft Word, Google Docs)

Word Processing Software like Microsoft Word or Google Docs is primarily designed for creating and formatting text documents, not for programming. However, these tools can be useful for documenting your code, writing technical specifications, and creating reports. Here's how you might use them for programming:

1. **Code Documentation:**
   - Write detailed explanations, comments, and documentation for your code in Word or Google Docs. This helps in understanding the purpose and functionality of your code.

2. **Technical Reports:**

   - Create technical reports or project documentation using Word or Google Docs to communicate your findings, challenges, and solutions.

3. **Pseudocode:**

   - Use these tools for drafting pseudocode or algorithm explanations before implementing them in your preferred programming environment.

4. **Collaboration:**

   - Share code snippets, explanations, or project details with team members through collaborative features in Google Docs or by attaching documents in email with Microsoft Word.

5. **Requirements and Planning:**

   - Document project requirements, specifications, and planning details using these tools for better organization and communication.

6. **Mockups and Diagrams:**

   - Insert diagrams, flowcharts, or mockups created in other tools to visually represent your program's structure or user interface.

7. **Table of Contents and Headings:**

   - Use the formatting features to create a structured document with a table of contents, headings, and subheadings for better readability.

Remember, while these tools are useful for documentation and collaboration, the actual coding and testing should be done in a dedicated integrated development environment (IDE) or code editor. Word Processing Software is not designed to execute or test code. Always ensure that your code is implemented and validated in a suitable programming environment.

3

Spreadsheet Software (e.g., Microsoft Excel, Google Sheets)

Spreadsheet software like Microsoft Excel or Google Sheets is not a traditional programming environment, but it can be leveraged for certain programming-related tasks, data analysis, and automation. Here's how you can use spreadsheet software for programming-related activities:

1. **Data Analysis and Visualization:**

   - Import your programming-related data into a spreadsheet and use built-in functions and charts to analyze and visualize the data.

2. **Formulae and Functions:**

   - Leverage formulas and functions to perform calculations on your data. Excel, for example, supports a variety of functions that can be used for statistical analysis, mathematical operations, and more.

3. **Automation with Macros:**

   - Excel and Google Sheets allow you to record and run macros, which are automated sequences of actions. While not as powerful as full-fledged programming, macros can automate repetitive tasks.

4. **Conditional Formatting:**

   - Use conditional formatting to highlight specific data points or apply formatting rules based on certain conditions.

5. **Data Manipulation:**

   - Manipulate and transform data using features like sorting, filtering, and pivot tables.

6. **Importing and Exporting Data:**

   - Import data from external sources into your spreadsheet for analysis. Similarly, you can export data to other formats.

7. **Prototyping and Planning:**

   - Plan and prototype algorithms or data structures in a more visual way, especially if your programming task involves numerical calculations or data manipulation.

8. **Collaboration:**

   - Collaborate with team members by sharing spreadsheets and allowing multiple users to work on them simultaneously.

9. **Simulation and Modeling:**

   - For certain simulations or modeling tasks, you can use spreadsheet software to implement simple models and observe changes over time.

10. **Data Validation:**

   - Implement data validation rules to ensure that your data adheres to specific criteria.

Remember that while spreadsheet software is versatile for data-related tasks, it has limitations compared to traditional programming environments. For more complex programming tasks, consider using a dedicated programming language and environment.

4

Presentation Software (e.g., Microsoft PowerPoint, Google Slides)

Presentation software like Microsoft PowerPoint or Google Slides is not intended for programming but can be employed for visually presenting programming-related content, project updates, or technical information. Here are ways you can use presentation software in a programming context:

1. **Code Presentation:**
   - Display code snippets, algorithms, or pseudocode on slides to explain your programming logic during presentations or meetings.

2. **Project Overview:**

   - Use slides to provide an overview of your programming project, including its goals, architecture, and key features.

3. **Flowcharts and Diagrams:**

   - Create flowcharts, diagrams, or UML diagrams to illustrate the structure and flow of your code or system.

4. **Code Reviews:**

   - Utilize slides to present code during code reviews, highlighting specific sections, changes, or improvements.

5. **API Documentation:**

   - Present API documentation, usage examples, and key functionalities using slides for better understanding.

6. **Bug Reports:**

   - Create slides to visually explain bugs, issues, or troubleshooting steps during discussions or presentations.

7. **Tech Talks and Workshops:**

   - Use presentations to conduct tech talks, workshops, or training sessions on programming topics.

8. **Demo and Showcase:**

   - Showcase your programming project or application through slides, providing a walkthrough of features and functionalities.

9. **Timeline and Milestones:**

   - Present the timeline of your programming project, including milestones, deadlines, and achievements.

10. **Integration with Other Tools:**

   - Embed screenshots, graphs, or charts generated from programming tools into your slides for visual representation.

11. **Collaboration:**

   - Collaborate with team members by sharing presentation files, allowing collaborative editing, and receiving feedback.

Remember that while presentation software is excellent for communication and visual representation, the actual programming work and testing should be done in a dedicated programming environment. Use these tools to complement your programming efforts and effectively communicate your ideas to a broader audience.

5

Web Browsers (e.g., Chrome, Firefox, Safari)

Web browsers like Chrome, Firefox, and Safari are essential tools for web developers and programmers. Here's how you can use web browsers for programming-related tasks:

1. **Web Development Tools:**
   - Browsers come with built-in developer tools (DevTools) that allow you to inspect and debug web pages, view network activity, and manipulate the DOM (Document Object Model).

2. **HTML/CSS/JavaScript Testing:**
   - Use browsers to test and debug HTML, CSS, and JavaScript code. DevTools provide a console for running JavaScript commands and seeing the output.

3. **Cross-Browser Testing:**

   - Test your websites or web applications on different browsers to ensure compatibility. Browsershots or services like BrowserStack can help with cross-browser testing.

4. **Extensions/Add-ons:**

   - Install browser extensions or add-ons that assist with development, such as ad blockers, color pickers, and code validators.

5. **AJAX and API Testing:**

   - Test and troubleshoot AJAX requests and APIs using browser tools. You can inspect network requests, check response data, and monitor API interactions.

6. **Responsive Design Testing:**

   - Use the browser's responsive design mode to test how your website or application looks on different devices and screen sizes.

7. **Local Development Servers:**

   - Set up a local development server to run and test your web applications locally before deploying them. Browsers can interact with these local servers.

8. **Performance Analysis:**

   - Use browser tools to analyze the performance of your web pages, identify bottlenecks, and optimize loading times.

9. **Browser Compatibility:**

   - Check for browser compatibility issues by manually testing your code on different browsers. Browsers provide a variety of tools to emulate different browser environments.

10. **Bookmarking and Documentation:**

   - Bookmark useful documentation, forums, and resources related to web development. Organize bookmarks for quick reference.

11. **Browser-Based IDEs:**

   - Explore browser-based integrated development environments (IDEs) like Repl.it or CodeSandbox for quick prototyping and collaborative coding.

12. **WebAssembly (Wasm) Development:**

   - Experiment with WebAssembly development directly in the browser, using tools like WasmFiddle or WebAssembly Studio.

13. **WebSocket and Real-Time Testing:**

   - Test WebSocket connections and real-time features using browser tools to inspect WebSocket frames and messages.

14. **Security Testing:**

   - Use browser extensions and tools to test the security of your web applications, such as checking for HTTPS implementation or identifying potential vulnerabilities.

Browsers are versatile tools for web development, offering a range of features to streamline coding, testing, and debugging processes. Incorporate these functionalities into your workflow to enhance your programming experience.

6

Antivirus Software (e.g., Norton, McAfee)

Antivirus software, such as Norton or McAfee, is primarily designed to protect your computer from malware, viruses, and other security threats. While they are not programming tools, there are certain considerations for using antivirus software in a programming environment:

1. **Scheduled Scans:**
   - Set up scheduled antivirus scans during periods when you are not actively using your computer. This helps ensure that your programming work is not disrupted by resource-intensive scans.

2. **Exclusions for Development Tools:**
   - Configure your antivirus software to exclude directories where your development tools, compilers, and IDEs store

files. This prevents false positives and enhances the performance of your development environment.

3. **Source Code Repositories:**

    - Add exclusions for directories where your source code repositories are stored. This helps prevent interference with version control systems like Git.

4. **Build Output Directories:**

    - Exclude directories where your build output is generated to avoid any conflicts during compilation.

5. **Configuration Files:**

    - Include exclusions for configuration files and settings related to your development tools to prevent false positives or interference with tool configurations.

6. **Update Definitions Regularly:**

    - Ensure that your antivirus software is regularly updated with the latest virus definitions to stay protected against emerging threats.

7. **Firewall Settings:**

    - If your antivirus software includes a firewall, configure it to allow traffic related to your programming tools and applications.

8. **Behavioral Analysis:**

   - Some antivirus solutions offer behavioral analysis. Understand how it works and customize settings to accommodate the behavior of your development tools.

9. **Temporary File Exclusions:**

   - Exclude directories where temporary files or caches used by your development tools are stored. This can prevent unnecessary scanning and potential performance issues.

10. **Suspend Scans During Intensive Tasks:**

    - If your antivirus software allows it, consider suspending scans during resource-intensive tasks such as compiling large projects to avoid performance slowdowns.

11. **Regular Backups:**

    - Regularly back up your important programming projects. In case of false positives or other issues, having a backup ensures you can recover your work.

12. **Documentation and Support:**

    - Familiarize yourself with the documentation and support resources provided by your antivirus software vendor. They often offer guidelines for configuring the software in development environments.

Remember that the specific steps may vary depending on the antivirus software you are using. Always consult the documentation provided by your antivirus software vendor for accurate and up-to-date information on configuration and exclusions.

7

Graphic Design Software (e.g., Adobe Photoshop, Canva)

Graphic Design Software (e.g., Adobe Photoshop, Canva)

Graphic design software, such as Adobe Photoshop or Canva, allows you to create and manipulate visual content. Here's a basic guide on how to use graphic design software:

Adobe Photoshop:

1. **Interface:**
   - Familiarize yourself with the Photoshop interface, including the toolbar, panels, and workspace.

2. **Canvas and Layers:**

   - Create a new document (canvas) and understand the concept of layers. Layers allow you to stack and organize different elements.

3. **Tools:**

   - Explore the various tools available, such as the selection tools, brushes, text tool, and more. Each tool serves a specific purpose.

4. **Image Editing:**

   - Use tools like the Brush, Eraser, and Clone Stamp for editing and retouching images.

5. **Filters and Effects:**

   - Apply filters and effects to enhance or alter your images. Photoshop offers a wide range of filters and adjustments.

6. **Text and Typography:**

   - Add text to your designs, customize fonts, sizes, and colors. Explore advanced typography features.

7. **Shapes and Drawing:**

   - Create shapes and draw freehand using the Pen tool or other shape tools.

8. **Masking and Blending:**

   - Learn about layer masking and blending modes to seamlessly integrate different elements.

9. **Export and Save:**

   - Understand how to save your work in different formats and export images for various purposes.

Canva:

1. **Sign Up and Choose a Template:**

   - Create an account on Canva and start by choosing a template that suits your design needs.

2. **Canvas and Elements:**

   - Understand the Canva workspace, including the canvas where you can drag and drop elements.

3. **Text and Typography:**

   - Add text to your designs using the text tool. Customize fonts, colors, and sizes easily.

4. **Images and Backgrounds:**

   - Import images or choose from Canva's library. Change backgrounds and adjust image properties.

5. **Elements and Icons:**

   - Explore the Elements tab to add icons, shapes, and other graphical elements to your design.

6. **Templates and Layouts:**

   - Modify pre-designed templates or create your layouts using Canva's extensive library of design elements.

7. **Collaboration:**

   - Canva allows collaboration with team members. Understand how to share, comment, and collaborate on designs.

8. **Export and Download:**

   - Once your design is complete, export it in various formats or download it directly from Canva.

Remember to consult the documentation or tutorials provided by each software to explore more advanced features. Both Adobe Photoshop and Canva have extensive communities and resources online to help you improve your graphic design skills. Practice and experimentation are key to becoming proficient with these tools.

8

Video Editing Software (e.g., Adobe Premiere Pro, iMovie)

Video Editing Software (e.g., Adobe Premiere Pro, iMovie)

Video editing software, such as Adobe Premiere Pro or iMovie, allows you to edit and enhance video content. Here's a basic guide on how to use video editing software:

Adobe Premiere Pro:

1. **Import Media:**
   - Start by importing your video clips, audio files, and any other media you want to include in your project.

2. **Timeline:**

   - Familiarize yourself with the timeline, where you arrange and edit your video clips. Understand the concept of tracks for video and audio.

3. **Basic Editing:**

   - Cut, trim, and arrange clips on the timeline. Use the razor tool to split clips and the selection tool to move and adjust them.

4. **Transitions:**

   - Add transitions between clips for smooth video flow. Premiere Pro provides various transition effects.

5. **Audio Editing:**

   - Adjust the volume levels, add background music, and synchronize audio with video. Apply audio effects as needed.

6. **Titles and Text:**

   - Insert titles, text overlays, and graphics. Customize fonts, colors, and animations.

7. **Effects and Color Correction:**

   - Apply video effects, color correction, and grading to enhance the visual appeal. Premiere Pro offers a wide range of effects and adjustment tools.

8. **Motion Graphics:**

   - Create and animate motion graphics using Premiere Pro's built-in tools or import graphics from Adobe After Effects.

9. **Export and Share:**

   - Once your video is edited, export it in the desired format and resolution. Premiere Pro provides various export settings to tailor output according to your needs.

iMovie:

1. **Create a New Project:**

   - Open iMovie and create a new project. Choose the appropriate aspect ratio and resolution for your video.

2. **Import Media:**

   - Import video clips, photos, and audio into your iMovie project.

3. **Timeline and Storyboard:**

   - Understand the timeline and storyboard where you arrange and edit your video clips. iMovie uses a simplified approach compared to professional software like Premiere Pro.

4. **Basic Editing:**

   - Cut, trim, and arrange clips on the timeline. iMovie provides easy drag-and-drop functionality for editing.

5. **Transitions and Effects:**

   - Add transitions between clips and apply video effects. iMovie has a collection of built-in effects and transitions.

6. **Audio Editing:**

   - Adjust audio levels, add background music, and apply audio effects. iMovie simplifies audio editing with straightforward controls.

7. **Titles and Text:**

   - Insert titles, text overlays, and credits. Customize fonts, colors, and animations.

8. **Export and Share:**

   - Export your edited video using iMovie's export feature. You can share directly to platforms like YouTube or save the video file locally.

Remember to consult the documentation or tutorials provided by each software for more advanced features. Both Adobe Premiere Pro and iMovie offer a range of tools for video editing, suitable for different skill levels and project requirements. Practice and experimentation will help you become more comfortable with these tools.

9

Database Management Software (e.g., MySQL, Microsoft Access)

Database management software, such as MySQL or Microsoft Access, allows you to create, organize, and manipulate databases. Here's a basic guide on how to use these types of database management software:

MySQL:

1. **Installation:**
   - Install MySQL on your machine. You can use MySQL's official website or package managers like apt or Homebrew.

2. **Database Creation:**
   - Use MySQL's command-line interface or a graphical tool like MySQL Workbench to create a new database.

```sql
CREATE DATABASE your_database_name;
```

3. **Table Creation:**
   - Create tables within the database to store your data.

```sql
CREATE TABLE your_table_name (
column1 datatype,
column2 datatype,
...
);
```

4. **Inserting Data:**
   - Insert data into your tables using the `INSERT INTO` statement.

```sql
INSERT INTO your_table_name (column1, column2, ...) VALUES (value1, value2, ...);
```

5. **Querying Data:**

   - Retrieve data from your tables using the `SELECT` statement.

```sql
   SELECT * FROM your_table_name;
```

6. **Updating Data:**

   - Update existing data in your tables with the `UPDATE` statement.

```sql
   UPDATE your_table_name SET column1 = new_value WHERE condition;
```

7. **Deleting Data:**

   - Remove data from your tables using the `DELETE` statement.

```sql
   DELETE FROM your_table_name WHERE condition;
```

8. **Indexes and Constraints:**

   - Implement indexes for efficient querying and enforce constraints (e.g., primary keys, foreign keys) to maintain data integrity.

9. **Backup and Restore:**

   - Regularly backup your database using tools like `mysqldump` and learn how to restore it if needed.

Microsoft Access:

1. **Database Creation:**

   - Launch Microsoft Access and create a new database file (.accdb).

2. **Table Design:**

   - Use the Table Design view to create tables by specifying field names, data types, and other properties.

3. **Data Entry:**

   - Switch to Datasheet View to enter data directly into your tables.

4. **Query Creation:**

   - Create queries to retrieve and manipulate data. Use the Query Design view to define criteria.

5. **Form Design:**

   - Design forms to create user-friendly interfaces for data entry or viewing.

6. **Report Design:**

   - Design reports to present data in a structured and printable format.

7. **Relationships:**

   - Establish relationships between tables to maintain referential integrity.

8. **Querying and Filtering:**

   - Use the built-in Query Wizard or SQL view to create more complex queries for data extraction.

9. **Export and Import Data:**

   - Export data to other formats (e.g., Excel) and import data from external sources.

10. **Backup and Compact:**

   - Regularly back up your Microsoft Access database and use the Compact and Repair Database option to optimize its performance.

Remember to consult the documentation provided by each software for more advanced features and capabilities. Database management involves careful planning and consideration of data relationships to ensure efficient and accurate data storage and retrieval.

10

Web Development Software (e.g., Sublime Text, Visual Studio Code)

Web development software, such as Sublime Text and Visual Studio Code, serves as code editors and IDEs for building websites and web applications. Here's a basic guide on how to use these popular web development tools:

Sublime Text:

1. **Installation:**
   - Download and install Sublime Text from the official website.

2. **Text Editing:**
   - Open files or create new ones for editing. Sublime Text provides a clean and minimalistic interface for coding.

3. **Syntax Highlighting:**

   - Benefit from syntax highlighting that makes different parts of your code visually distinct and easier to read.

4. **Packages and Extensions:**

   - Explore and install packages or extensions for additional functionalities. Sublime Text has a vibrant package ecosystem.

5. **Multi-Cursor Editing:**

   - Use multi-cursor editing to edit multiple occurrences of a selection simultaneously, improving efficiency.

6. **Command Palette:**

   - Access various commands, settings, and package features through the Command Palette (Ctrl + Shift + P).

7. **Themes and Color Schemes:**

   - Customize the appearance of Sublime Text with themes and color schemes available in the preferences.

8. **Multiple Panes:**

   - Split your view into multiple panes to work on different parts of the code simultaneously.

Visual Studio Code (VSCode):

1. **Installation:**
   - Download and install Visual Studio Code from the official website.

2. **Extensions:**
   - Install extensions to enhance VSCode's functionality. Extensions cover themes, debugging tools, language support, and more.

3. **Integrated Terminal:**
   - Utilize the integrated terminal for running commands directly within VSCode.

4. **Version Control Integration:**
   - Benefit from built-in version control integration (e.g., Git) to track changes and manage collaboration.

5. **Debugging:**
   - Set breakpoints and debug your code directly within VSCode, making it a powerful tool for troubleshooting.

6. **IntelliSense:**
   - Leverage IntelliSense for autocompletion and contextual suggestions while writing code.

7. **Live Server Extension:**

   - Install extensions like Live Server to create a local development server and see changes in real-time.

8. **Task Runner:**

   - Define and run tasks using the built-in task runner for common build processes.

9. **Code Formatting:**

   - Use the built-in or extension-supported code formatting tools to maintain consistent code styling.

10. **Themes and Color Customization:**

    - Personalize the appearance with different themes and color customization options available in the preferences.

Both Sublime Text and Visual Studio Code are highly extensible and can be tailored to fit various web development needs. Explore their features, customize settings to match your preferences, and integrate extensions that enhance your workflow. Each tool has a vast community and documentation resources available for more in-depth exploration.

11

Audio Editing Software (e.g., Audacity, GarageBand)

Audio editing software, such as Audacity or GarageBand, allows you to manipulate and enhance audio recordings. Here's a basic guide on how to use these popular audio editing tools:

Audacity:

1. **Installation:**
   - Download and install Audacity from the official website.

2. **Import Audio:**
   - Open Audacity and import an audio file or record a new one using the built-in recording feature.

3. **Editing Tools:**

   - Familiarize yourself with editing tools like Cut, Copy, Paste, and Delete for basic audio editing.

4. **Selection and Zoom:**

   - Use selection tools to highlight portions of the audio for editing. Zoom in and out to navigate through the waveform.

5. **Effects:**

   - Explore the Effects menu to apply various audio effects such as amplification, equalization, and noise reduction.

6. **Multitrack Editing:**

   - Create multitrack projects to combine multiple audio sources or layer different elements.

7. **Generate and Analyze:**

   - Use the Generate menu to create tones, silence, or other audio elements. Analyze features include spectrum analysis and pitch detection.

8. **Export and Save:**

   - Save your project in Audacity's native format (.aup) and export the final audio in various formats such as MP3 or WAV.

GarageBand:

1. **Installation:**
   - GarageBand comes pre-installed on macOS devices. For iOS devices, it can be downloaded from the App Store.

2. **Create a New Project:**
   - Launch GarageBand and create a new audio project. Choose the appropriate project type (e.g., Voice, Music).

3. **Tracks and Regions:**
   - Add tracks to your project to represent different audio elements. Arrange audio regions on the tracks for editing.

4. **Editing Tools:**
   - Familiarize yourself with editing tools like Cut, Copy, Paste, and Split for basic audio editing.

5. **Real-Time Effects:**
   - Apply real-time effects like reverb, echo, and equalization to individual tracks or the entire project.

6. **Software Instruments:**
   - GarageBand includes software instruments. Explore the library of virtual instruments and create MIDI-based music.

7. **Smart Controls:**

   - Use Smart Controls to manipulate the sound of your software instruments and adjust various parameters.

8. **Automation:**

   - Automate volume, pan, and other parameters over time to add dynamic changes to your audio.

9. **Export and Share:**

   - Save your GarageBand project and export the final audio file in various formats.

Remember to consult the documentation or tutorials provided by each software for more advanced features and capabilities. Both Audacity and GarageBand are powerful tools for audio editing and are suitable for a wide range of projects, from simple voice recordings to more complex music production. Practice and experimentation will help you become more proficient with these tools.

12

Content Management System (CMS) (e.g., WordPress, Joomla)

Content Management Systems (CMS), like WordPress or Joomla, simplify the process of creating and managing websites. Here's a basic guide on how to use these popular CMS platforms:

WordPress:

1. **Installation:**
   - Install WordPress on your web server or use a local server environment for testing.

2. **Login to Dashboard:**
   - Access the WordPress admin dashboard by appending `/wp-admin` to your site's URL (e.g., `yoursite.com/wp-admin`). Log in with your credentials.

3. **Themes:**

- Choose a theme to determine the look and feel of your website. Install and customize themes from the WordPress Theme Directory or third-party providers.

4. **Plugins:**

- Enhance functionality with plugins. Install plugins to add features like contact forms, SEO tools, or e-commerce capabilities.

5. **Pages and Posts:**

- Create pages for static content (e.g., About Us, Contact) and posts for dynamic content like blog entries.

6. **Media Library:**

- Upload and manage media files (images, videos, documents) in the Media Library. Easily insert them into pages or posts.

7. **Categories and Tags:**

- Organize content using categories and tags. Assign relevant categories and tags to your posts for better navigation.

8. **Menus:**

   - Customize navigation menus. Create and edit menus to include pages, categories, or custom links.

9. **Widgets:**

   - Use widgets to add additional content and features to sidebars or other widget areas.

10. **User Management:**

   - Manage user roles and permissions. Control who can contribute, edit, or manage the website.

11. **Settings:**

   - Configure general settings such as site title, tagline, and timezone. Adjust reading, writing, and discussion settings.

12. **Updates:**

   - Regularly update WordPress core, themes, and plugins to ensure security and access new features.

Joomla:

1. **Installation:**

   - Install Joomla on your web server or use a local server environment for testing.

2. **Login to Administrator Panel:**

   - Access the Joomla administrator panel by appending `/administrator` to your site's URL (e.g., `yoursite.com/administrator`). Log in with your credentials.

3. **Templates:**

   - Choose a template to determine your website's layout and design. Install and customize templates from the Joomla Extensions Directory.

4. **Extensions:**

   - Enhance functionality with extensions. Install extensions to add features like galleries, forums, or e-commerce capabilities.

5. **Articles and Categories:**

   - Create articles for your website's content. Organize articles into categories for better structure.

6. **Menus:**

   - Create menus to navigate through your website. Assign articles or categories to menu items.

7. **Modules and Positions:**

   - Use modules to add content or features to specific positions on your site (e.g., sidebar, footer).

8. **Components:**

   - Components are major extensions that often have their menu items and pages. Examples include contact forms, search, or news feeds.

9. **Global Configuration:**

   - Configure global settings such as site name, metadata, and SEO settings in the Global Configuration.

10. **User Management:**

   - Manage user groups and permissions. Control who can contribute, edit, or manage the website.

11. **Languages:**

   - Joomla supports multiple languages. Configure language settings and manage multilingual content.

12. **Updates:**

   - Regularly update Joomla core, templates, and extensions to ensure security and access new features.

Remember to consult the documentation and tutorials provided by each CMS for more advanced features and capabilities. Both WordPress and Joomla have active communities and extensive resources available for further exploration and troubleshooting. Practice and experimentation will help you become more comfortable with using these CMS platforms.

58

13

Customer Relationship Management (CRM) Software (e.g., Salesforce, HubSpot)

Customer Relationship Management (CRM) software, such as Salesforce or HubSpot, helps businesses manage interactions with their customers and streamline various processes. Here's a basic guide on how to use these popular CRM platforms:

Salesforce:

1. **User Setup:**
   - Set up user accounts for your team members with the necessary permissions. Define roles and profiles to control access.

2. **Contact Management:**

   - Add and manage customer contacts in Salesforce. Capture essential information such as names, email addresses, and phone numbers.

3. **Lead Management:**

   - Use leads to track potential customers. Qualify leads, convert them into contacts, and associate them with accounts.

4. **Opportunity Management:**

   - Manage sales opportunities. Create opportunities, track their progress, and associate them with relevant accounts and contacts.

5. **Account Management:**

   - Organize and manage customer accounts. Keep track of account details, activities, and interactions.

6. **Activity Tracking:**

   - Log and track activities such as emails, calls, and meetings related to customers. Use the Activity Timeline to get a comprehensive view.

7. **Dashboards and Reports:**
   - Create dashboards and reports to analyze data. Visualize key metrics and gain insights into your sales and customer interactions.

8. **Automation:**
   - Implement automation workflows for routine tasks. Use Process Builder or Workflow Rules to automate processes and save time.

9. **Integration with Email and Calendar:**
   - Integrate Salesforce with your email and calendar applications. Log emails and schedule appointments directly within Salesforce.

10. **Customization:**
   - Customize Salesforce to fit your business needs. Create custom fields, page layouts, and record types.

HubSpot:

1. **User Setup:**
   - Set up user accounts in HubSpot with appropriate roles and permissions. Define team members' access to different features.

2. **Contact Management:**

   - Manage customer contacts in HubSpot. Capture and store contact details, interactions, and engagement history.

3. **Lead Capture:**

   - Use lead capture forms on your website to gather information about potential customers. Automatically create contacts in HubSpot.

4. **Deal and Pipeline Management:**

   - Manage sales deals and organize them into pipelines. Track deal stages, values, and associated contacts.

5. **Company Records:**

   - Keep track of company details, interactions, and relationships. Associate contacts and deals with relevant companies.

6. **Email Marketing:**

   - Use HubSpot's email marketing tools to create and send targeted email campaigns. Track engagement and analyze campaign performance.

7. **Marketing Automation:**

   - Set up marketing automation workflows to nurture leads, send follow-up emails, and automate marketing tasks.

8. **Social Media Integration:**

   - Integrate social media accounts to monitor and engage with your audience directly within HubSpot.

9. **Reports and Analytics:**

   - Generate reports and analytics to evaluate the performance of your marketing and sales efforts. Gain insights into customer behavior.

10. **Customization:**

   - Customize HubSpot to align with your business processes. Configure custom properties, workflows, and templates.

Remember to consult the documentation and tutorials provided by each CRM platform for more advanced features and capabilities. Both Salesforce and HubSpot offer extensive resources, training, and community support to help users make the most of their CRM tools. Practice and experimentation will help you become more proficient with these   platforms.

14

Project Management Software (e.g., Trello, Asana)

Project Management Software, such as Trello or Asana, helps teams organize tasks, collaborate, and track project progress. Here's a basic guide on how to use these popular project management tools:

Trello:

1. **Board Creation:**
   - Create a new board for each project. Boards act as the main organizational units.

2. **Lists:**
   - Within each board, create lists to represent different stages or phases of your project (e.g., To Do, In Progress, Done).

3. **Cards:**

   - Use cards to represent individual tasks or items. Create cards within lists and add details, descriptions, due dates, and attachments.

4. **Labels:**

   - Apply labels to cards for categorization or to highlight specific attributes (e.g., priority, type of task).

5. **Attachments:**

   - Attach files directly to cards. Share relevant documents, images, or links related to the task.

6. **Comments:**

   - Use the comment section within cards for team communication and updates. Mention team members to notify them.

7. **Checklists:**

   - Add checklists to cards to break down tasks into smaller, manageable sub-tasks.

8. **Due Dates:**

   - Assign due dates to cards to ensure tasks are completed on time. Set reminders for upcoming deadlines.

9. **Activity Feed:**

   - Review the activity feed to see changes, comments, and progress made on the board.

10. **Power-Ups:**

   - Explore and enable Power-Ups to extend Trello's functionality. Power-Ups can integrate Trello with other tools and add features like calendars and voting.

Asana:

1. **Workspace and Project Creation:**

   - Create a workspace for your organization or team. Within the workspace, create projects to represent different initiatives.

2. **Tasks:**

   - Break down work into tasks. Create tasks within projects and add details such as assignees, due dates, and descriptions.

3. **Sections and Columns:**

   - Use sections or columns to organize tasks within a project. Sections help group related tasks together.

4. **Board View:**

   - Switch to the board view to see tasks organized in columns. Move tasks between columns to represent progress.

5. **Milestones:**

   - Use milestones to mark significant points in your project. Milestones help track progress and celebrate achievements.

6. **Dependencies:**

   - Set task dependencies to indicate the order in which tasks should be completed. Ensure that one task doesn't start until another is finished.

7. **Attachments and Comments:**

   - Attach files to tasks and use the comment section for team collaboration. Mention teammates to notify them of updates.

8. **Calendar View:**

   - Switch to the calendar view to visualize project timelines and due dates.

9. **Dashboards and Reports:**

   - Create dashboards and reports to track project progress, team workload, and completion rates.

10. **Integrations:**

   - Integrate Asana with other tools and apps your team uses, such as Slack, Google Drive, or Microsoft Teams.

Remember to consult the documentation and tutorials provided by each project management tool for more advanced features and capabilities. Both Trello and Asana offer various collaboration and planning features that can be customized to fit your team's workflow. Practice and experimentation will help you become more proficient with these tools.

15

Accounting Software (e.g., QuickBooks, Xero)

Accounting software, such as QuickBooks or Xero, helps businesses manage their financial transactions, invoices, and overall financial health. Here's a basic guide on how to use these popular accounting tools:

QuickBooks:

1. **Account Setup:**
   - Set up your business accounts in QuickBooks. This includes bank accounts, income, and expense categories.

2. **Chart of Accounts:**
   - Customize your chart of accounts to match your business structure. This helps organize financial transactions.

3. **Connect Bank and Credit Card Accounts:**

   - Connect your bank and credit card accounts to QuickBooks for automatic transaction importing. This simplifies reconciliation.

4. **Invoicing:**

   - Create and send professional invoices to your customers. Customize invoice templates and set up payment terms.

5. **Expense Tracking:**

   - Record and categorize your business expenses. Attach receipts for documentation.

6. **Bank Reconciliation:**

   - Regularly reconcile your bank and credit card accounts with QuickBooks to ensure accurate financial records.

7. **Financial Reports:**

   - Generate financial reports such as profit and loss statements, balance sheets, and cash flow statements for insights into your business's financial health.

8. **Payroll:**

- Use QuickBooks Payroll to manage employee compensation, taxes, and benefits. Ensure compliance with payroll regulations.

9. **Sales Tax:**

- Set up and manage sales tax in QuickBooks. Automatically calculate and track sales tax on transactions.

10. **Budgeting:**

- Create budgets in QuickBooks to plan and monitor your business's financial performance against set targets.

Xero:

1. **Account Setup:**

- Set up your business in Xero by entering basic information about your organization.

2. **Chart of Accounts:**

- Customize your chart of accounts to align with your business structure and financial reporting needs.

3. **Bank Feeds:**

- Connect your bank accounts to Xero for automatic bank feeds. This simplifies the reconciliation process.

4. **Invoicing:**

   - Create professional invoices in Xero and send them directly to your clients. Customize invoice templates to match your brand.

5. **Expense Claims:**

   - Manage employee expense claims in Xero. Capture and reimburse business-related expenses.

6. **Bank Reconciliation:**

   - Reconcile your bank transactions in Xero regularly to ensure accuracy and completeness.

7. **Financial Reports:**

   - Generate financial reports such as profit and loss statements, balance sheets, and cash flow reports for comprehensive financial analysis.

8. **Payroll:**

   - Use Xero Payroll to manage employee payroll, including tax calculations and compliance.

9. **Sales Tax:**

   - Set up and manage sales tax in Xero. Ensure compliance with tax regulations and track tax liabilities.

10. **Budgeting:**

   - Create and monitor budgets in Xero to plan and assess your business's financial performance against targets.

Remember to consult the documentation and tutorials provided by each accounting software for more advanced features and capabilities. Both QuickBooks and Xero offer extensive support resources to help users effectively manage their business finances. Regularly update your financial records, reconcile accounts, and leverage reporting tools to make informed financial decisions.

16

Virtualization Software (e.g., VMware, VirtualBox)

Virtualization software, such as VMware or VirtualBox, allows you to run multiple operating systems on a single physical machine. Here's a basic guide on how to use these popular virtualization tools:

VMware:

1. **Installation:**

   - Download and install VMware Workstation on your host machine.

2. **Create a Virtual Machine (VM):**

   - Open VMware Workstation and click on "Create a New Virtual Machine." Follow the wizard to set up the VM, including selecting the operating system and specifying resources like CPU, RAM, and storage.

3. **Install Operating System:**

   - Install the guest operating system on the VM. This involves inserting the installation media (e.g., ISO file) and going through the installation process within the virtual environment.

4. **VM Settings:**

   - Adjust VM settings as needed. You can modify hardware configurations, add/remove virtual devices, and allocate more resources.

5. **Snapshots:**

   - Take snapshots of your VM at different points in time. Snapshots allow you to revert to a previous state if needed.

6. **Networking:**

   - Configure network settings for the VM. Choose between NAT, Bridged, or Host-Only networking options to define how the VM connects to the network.

7. **VMware Tools:**

   - Install VMware Tools within the guest operating system. VMware Tools enhances performance and allows seamless integration between the host and guest.

8. **Cloning and Templates:**

   - Clone existing VMs to create duplicates or use templates to streamline the VM creation process.

9. **Unity Mode (Optional):**

   - If using VMware Workstation on Windows, Unity mode allows you to run applications from the virtual machine directly on the host desktop.

VirtualBox:

1. **Installation:**

   - Download and install Oracle VM VirtualBox on your host machine.

2. **Create a Virtual Machine (VM):**

   - Open VirtualBox and click on "New" to create a new VM. Follow the wizard to set up the VM, including selecting the operating system and configuring resources.

3. **Install Operating System:**

   - Install the guest operating system on the VM. Similar to VMware, this involves using installation media (e.g., ISO file) to set up the OS within the virtual environment.

4. **VM Settings:**

   - Adjust VM settings using the VirtualBox Manager. Modify hardware configurations, add/remove virtual devices, and allocate more resources.

5. **Snapshots:**

   - Take snapshots of your VM to capture its current state. Snapshots allow you to roll back to a specific point in time.

6. **Networking:**

   - Configure network settings for the VM. VirtualBox offers various network modes, including NAT, Bridged, and Host-Only.

7. **Guest Additions:**

   - Install Guest Additions within the guest operating system. Guest Additions enhance performance and enable features like seamless mouse integration and shared folders.

8. **Cloning and Templates:**

   - Clone VMs to create duplicates or use the template feature for quicker VM creation.

Both VMware and VirtualBox provide extensive documentation and user guides. Additionally, online communities and forums are valuable resources for troubleshooting and advanced configurations. Experimentation and practice will enhance your proficiency in using virtualization software.

17

Communication and Collaboration Software (e.g., Slack, Microsoft Teams)

Communication and collaboration software, such as Slack or Microsoft Teams, facilitates team communication, file sharing, and collaboration. Here's a basic guide on how to use these popular tools:

Slack:

1. **Workspace Creation:**
   - Create a Slack workspace for your team. Invite team members to join the workspace.

2. **Channels:**

   - Organize discussions into channels based on topics, projects, or departments. Use public channels for open discussions and private channels for sensitive topics.

3. **Direct Messages:**

   - Send direct messages to individual team members for private conversations. You can also create group messages for multiple participants.

4. **Mentions and Notifications:**

   - Use mentions (@username) to get someone's attention. Adjust notification preferences to control how and when you receive alerts.

5. **File Sharing:**

   - Share files, images, and documents directly in Slack. Files can be uploaded to channels or sent in direct messages.

6. **Integrations:**

   - Integrate third-party apps and services to enhance Slack's functionality. Connect tools like Google Drive, Trello, or GitHub to streamline workflows.

7. **Slackbot:**

   - Utilize Slackbot for custom reminders, automation, and to answer frequently asked questions within your team.

8. **Threads:**

   - Keep conversations organized by using threads for replies to specific messages. Threads help reduce clutter in the main channel.

9. **Custom Emoji and Reactions:**

   - Add custom emoji reactions to messages for quick feedback or expressions. Customize your workspace with emojis that suit your team culture.

10. **Search and Archives:**

   - Easily search for messages, files, or conversations using Slack's search feature. Archived channels and messages are accessible for reference.

Microsoft Teams:

1. **Team Creation:**

   - Create a Microsoft Teams team for your organization or project. Add team members to collaborate within the team.

2. **Channels:**

   - Organize discussions into channels within a team. Use standard channels for broad topics and private channels for more focused conversations.

3. **Chat:**

   - Initiate one-on-one or group chats within Teams. Share messages, files, and multimedia directly in the chat.

4. **Meetings:**

   - Schedule and host meetings within Teams. Conduct video or audio calls, share screens, and collaborate in real-time.

5. **Files and SharePoint Integration:**

   - Share files within Teams and leverage SharePoint for document storage. Collaborate on files in real-time using Office 365 applications.

6. **Apps and Tabs:**

   - Add apps and tabs to your Teams channels to integrate external tools and services. Bring in data from Microsoft 365 apps or connect to third-party apps.

7. **Planner and To-Do Integration:**

   - Use Planner and To-Do integration to manage tasks, assign responsibilities, and track progress within Teams.

8. **@Mentions and Notifications:**

   - Use @mentions to notify specific team members in conversations. Adjust notification settings to receive alerts based on your preferences.

9. **Activity Feed:**

   - Keep track of updates and mentions in your activity feed. Stay informed about recent conversations and activities within Teams.

10. **Search and Archives:**

   - Search for messages, files, or content within Teams. Archived channels and messages are accessible for historical reference.

Both Slack and Microsoft Teams offer extensive user guides and help documentation. Experiment with features, utilize integrations that fit your workflow, and encourage team members to explore and contribute to the platform. Consistent usage and engagement will help your team maximize the benefits of these communication and collaboration tools.

18

GIS (Geographic Information System) Software (e.g., ArcGIS, QGIS)

Geographic Information System (GIS) software, such as ArcGIS or QGIS, allows users to analyze and visualize spatial data. Here's a basic guide on how to use these popular GIS tools:

ArcGIS:

1. **ArcGIS Online:**
   - Explore ArcGIS Online, a cloud-based platform that offers access to maps, apps, and data layers. You can create an account and start working with maps immediately.

2. **ArcGIS Desktop:**

   - Download and install ArcGIS Desktop for more advanced GIS capabilities. It includes ArcMap for 2D mapping and ArcScene/ArcGlobe for 3D mapping.

3. **Create a Map:**

   - Open ArcGIS Desktop and create a new map. Add data layers, such as shapefiles or CSV files containing geographic information.

4. **Symbolization:**

   - Customize the appearance of your map by symbolizing features based on attributes. Modify colors, sizes, and shapes of symbols.

5. **Geoprocessing Tools:**

   - Use geoprocessing tools to analyze spatial data. These tools perform operations such as buffering, overlay analysis, and spatial statistics.

6. **Map Layout:**

   - Design the layout of your map, including titles, legends, and scale bars. Prepare your map for printing or sharing.

7. **ArcGIS Pro (Optional):**

   - Explore ArcGIS Pro, the next-generation desktop GIS application. It provides a modern interface and enhanced 2D and 3D mapping capabilities.

8. **Web Maps and Apps:**

   - Share your maps as web maps and create web apps using ArcGIS Online. Publish your work for wider access and collaboration.

QGIS:

1. **Installation:**

   - Download and install QGIS on your computer. QGIS is an open-source GIS software available for various operating systems.

2. **Create a Project:**

   - Open QGIS and create a new project. Add layers to your project by loading shapefiles, raster images, or other data sources.

3. **Symbolization:**

   - Customize the appearance of map features by symbolizing them based on attributes. Adjust colors, styles, and labels.

4. **Attribute Tables:**

   - Access attribute tables to view and edit the non-spatial data associated with map features.

5. **Processing Toolbox:**

   - Utilize the Processing Toolbox for geoprocessing tasks. QGIS provides a wide range of tools for spatial analysis and data manipulation.

6. **Print Layout:**

   - Design the layout of your map for printing or exporting. Include elements like legends, scale bars, and titles.

7. **Plugins:**

   - Explore and install plugins to extend QGIS functionality. Plugins can provide additional tools, data sources, and visualization options.

8. **3D Visualization (Optional):**

   - QGIS supports 3D visualization. Use the QGIS 3D Viewer plugin to create and explore three-dimensional maps.

9. **Export and Share:**

   - Export your map as an image, PDF, or other formats. Share your QGIS projects or maps with others.

Remember to consult the documentation and tutorials provided by each GIS software for more advanced features and capabilities. Both ArcGIS and QGIS have active communities, forums, and extensive documentation that can assist users in mastering these powerful GIS tools. Practice and experimentation with spatial data will enhance your proficiency in GIS analysis and mapping.

19

E-commerce Platform (e.g., Shopify, Magento)

E-commerce platforms like Shopify and Magento enable businesses to set up and manage online stores. Here's a basic guide on how to use these popular e-commerce tools:

Shopify:

1. **Account Setup:**
   - Sign up for a Shopify account. Choose a unique store name and provide neccessary information to create your online store.

2. **Store Configuration:**
   - Customize your store settings, including currency, shipping, taxes, and payment methods in the Shopify admin dashboard.

3. **Product Management:**

   - Add products to your store. Include product details, images, prices, and variants. Organize products into categories and collections.

4. **Themes:**

   - Choose a Shopify theme or design your own to give your store a unique look. Customize colors, fonts, and layout to match your brand.

5. **Apps:**

   - Explore and install Shopify apps from the Shopify App Store to enhance your store's functionality. Apps can add features like customer reviews, social media integration, and more.

6. **Orders and Payments:**

   - Manage orders through the Shopify admin. Process payments, track shipments, and handle customer communications.

7. **Discounts and Promotions:**

   - Create discounts, promo codes, and special offers to attract customers. Set up sales and discounts directly in the admin.

8. **Analytics:**

   - Monitor your store's performance using Shopify's analytics tools. Track sales, customer behavior, and other key metrics.

9. **SEO Optimization:**

   - Optimize your store for search engines. Customize meta titles, descriptions, and URLs to improve your store's visibility.

10. **Mobile App (Optional):**

   - Download and use the Shopify mobile app to manage your store on the go. Monitor sales, update products, and respond to customer inquiries.

Magento:

1. **Magento Installation:**

   - Install Magento on your web server. You can choose the open-source version (Magento Community Edition) or the enterprise version (Magento Commerce).

2. **Store Configuration:**

   - Configure your store settings, including currencies, shipping methods, taxes, and payment gateways, through the Magento admin panel.

3. **Product Management:**

   - Add products to your store with detailed information, images, prices, and inventory tracking. Organize products into categories and attributes.

4. **Themes and Customization:**

   - Choose a Magento theme or create a custom theme to personalize your store's appearance. Customize layouts, colors, and styles.

5. **Extensions:**

   - Enhance your store's functionality by installing extensions from the Magento Marketplace. Extensions can add features like advanced search, social media integration, and more.

6. **Orders and Payments:**

   - Manage orders, process payments, and handle shipping through the Magento admin panel. Keep track of order statuses and customer communications.

7. **Promotions and Discounts:**

   - Create promotions, discounts, and special offers directly in Magento. Set up rules for discounts based on conditions like order amount or product categories.

8. **Analytics:**

   - Use built-in analytics tools or integrate third-party analytics solutions to track your store's performance. Monitor sales, customer behavior, and other metrics.

9. **SEO Optimization:**

   - Optimize your Magento store for search engines. Customize meta tags, URLs, and other SEO elements to improve your store's visibility.

10. **Mobile Responsiveness:**

   - Ensure your Magento store is mobile-friendly. Test and optimize the user experience on various devices.

Remember to consult the documentation and user guides provided by each e-commerce platform for more in-depth instructions and troubleshooting. Both Shopify and Magento offer extensive resources and community support to help users effectively manage and optimize their online stores. Regularly update your products, monitor analytics, and stay engaged with your customers for a successful e-commerce experience.

20

3D Modeling Software (e.g., AutoCAD, Blender)

3D modeling software allows you to create three-dimensional objects or scenes. Here's a basic guide on how to use two popular 3D modeling tools: AutoCAD and Blender.

AutoCAD:

1. **Interface Familiarization:**
   - Understand the AutoCAD interface, including the ribbon, command line, and drawing area.

2. **Drawing Tools:**
   - Use basic drawing tools like Line, Circle, and Rectangle to create 2D shapes.

3. **Extrusion and Elevation:**
   - Extrude 2D shapes to create 3D objects. Adjust elevations to give height to your drawings.

4. **Modify Commands:**

   - Master Modify commands like Move, Copy, Rotate, and Scale to manipulate objects.

5. **Layers:**

   - Organize your drawing using layers. Assign objects to different layers for better management.

6. **3D Modeling Workspace:**

   - Switch to the 3D Modeling workspace in AutoCAD for specialized tools and features.

7. **Solid Modeling:**

   - Explore solid modeling techniques to create complex 3D shapes. Use commands like Extrude, Union, and Subtract.

8. **Materials and Textures:**

   - Apply materials and textures to your 3D models to enhance realism.

9. **Viewports:**

   - Utilize multiple viewports to see different perspectives of your 3D model simultaneously.

10. **Rendering:**

   - Learn the basics of rendering. Adjust lighting, shadows, and rendering settings for a realistic visualization of your model.

Blender:

1. **Interface Familiarization:**

   - Understand the Blender interface, including the 3D View, Properties Panel, and Outliner.

2. **Mesh Modeling:**

   - Start with basic mesh modeling. Use tools like Add, Extrude, and Scale to create 3D objects.

3. **Modifiers:**

   - Explore modifiers to add complexity and details to your models. Common modifiers include Subdivision Surface and Bevel.

4. **UV Mapping:**

   - Understand UV mapping to apply textures accurately to your 3D models.

5. **Sculpting (Optional):**
   - Blender includes sculpting tools for organic modeling. Use brushes to mold and shape surfaces.

6. **Materials and Shading:**
   - Create materials and shading in Blender's Shader Editor. Adjust properties like color, roughness, and metallicness.

7. **Animation (Optional):**
   - Blender is capable of animation. Learn the basics of keyframing, timelines, and the Graph Editor.

8. **Particle Systems (Optional):**
   - Experiment with particle systems to simulate effects like fire, smoke, or hair.

9. **Camera and Lighting:**
   - Set up cameras and lights to compose scenes. Adjust lighting properties for realistic renders.

10. **Rendering:**
   - Use Blender's Cycles or Eevee render engines to create high-quality renders. Adjust render settings for optimal results.

Both AutoCAD and Blender have extensive documentation, tutorials, and online communities. Experiment with these tools, follow tutorials, and gradually take on more complex projects to improve your 3D modeling skills. Practicing regularly will enhance your proficiency and creativity in using 3D modeling software.

Digitales Gold: Online Geld verdienen leicht gemacht

Alexander Müller